Make and Take Your Own

by Gemma Ridgway-Faye

Make Your Own

You can make your own food. It is good for you and the planet.

You could make a snack plate. Chop up raw sticks to have with dip.

You could make a carrot cake.

Pop the mix in a round cake tin.

Bake a cake and cut it up.

You can **flaunt** your skills.

Take it to the backyard.

You can make your own drink in the blender. Mix a banana, seeds and milk.

This is a milkshake.

You do not need these in your trolley.

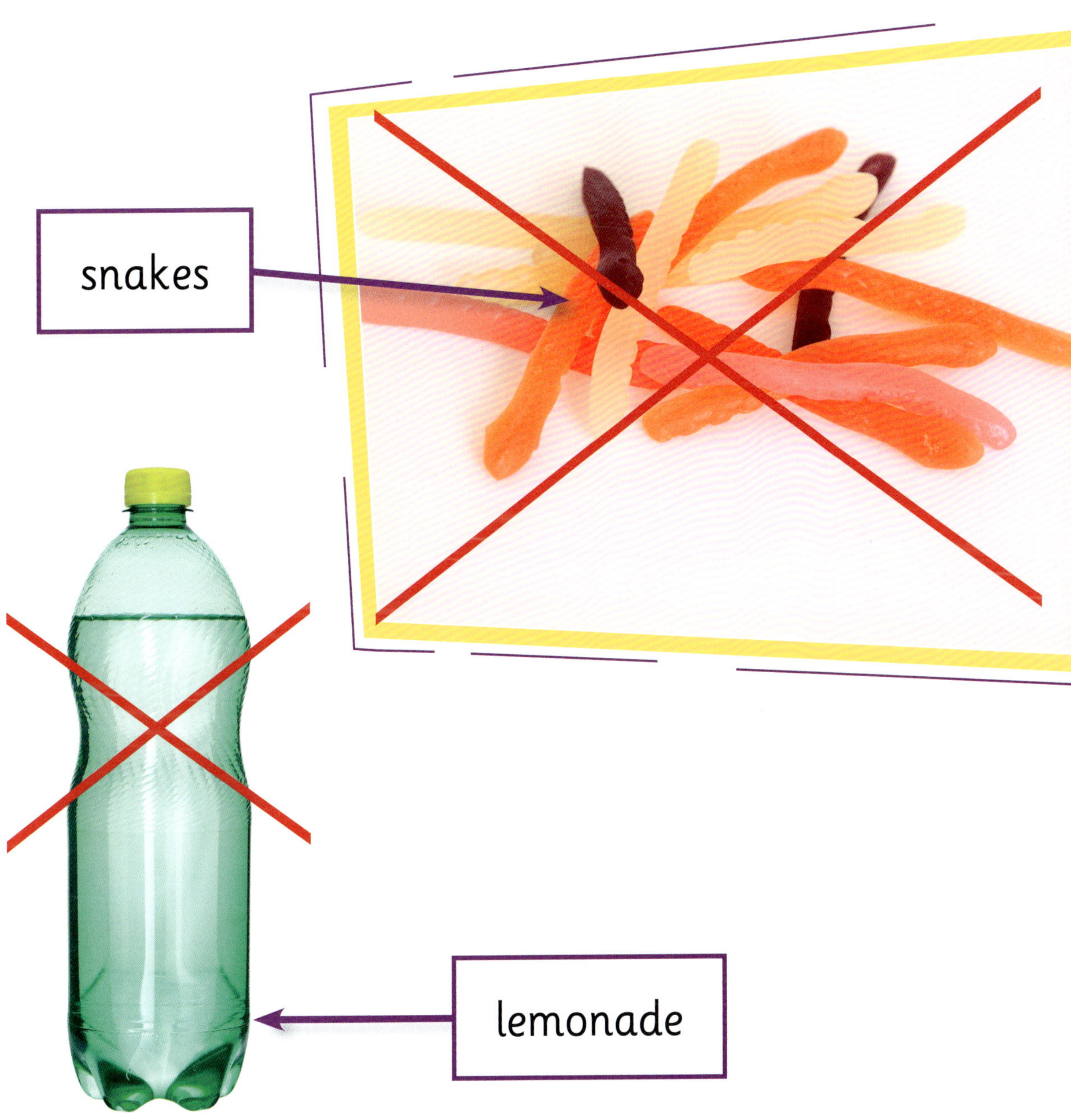

Make dinner at your house in the evening. It is better than takeaway.

You can even help to cook. Think of a dish you might like to make.

You could bake some fish. Add lemon and dill on top. You could add salad.

You could make a pie. Add some beans and corn.

It's a perfect meal for winter.

These are soft and sweet pancakes. The peaches are hot and gooey.

You can help clean up once the meal is finished.

Clear the plates.

Save the uneaten food.

Pull the beeswax taut to keep it fresh.

Scrape the plates.

Food scraps go in the **compost**.

Take Your Own

You can pack your own lunch. Take what you love to eat.

Aim to make less **litter**. Say no to plastic.

No packet means less rubbish.

Make a sandwich with turkey. Add some greens or an egg.

Put the snacks in a separate part.

These are a fun shape.

When you go out, you might need a drink. Take your own water bottle with you.

Take your own cup with a lid. It will be safe and will not spill.

Big Impact

Do you make your own food? Do you take a water bottle with you?

See if you can make and take your own. Little steps make a big **impact**.

Look It Up

compost: leftover food for garden soil

flaunt: show off

impact: change or affect something

litter: rubbish

Index